Squirrels
For Kids

Amazing Animal Books
For Young Readers

By
Rachel Smith

Mendon Cottage Books

JD-Biz Publishing

Read More Amazing Animal Books

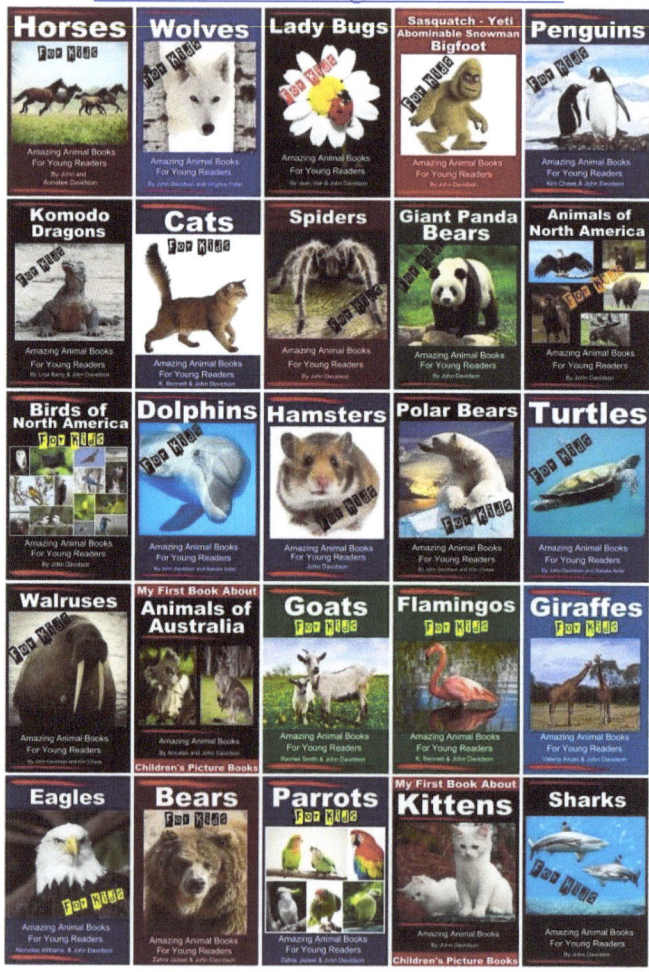

Purchase at Amazon.com

Table of Contents

Introduction

Squirrels are cute little critters we see running around our forests and sometimes our backyards. With their fluffy tails and small bodies, they have enchanted many writers and storytellers.

From the nimble squirrel fighters in the *Redwall* series by Brian Jacques to Nutkin from the Beatrix Potter book, squirrels are generally portrayed well, even if sometimes they can be a little dumb.

Some people don't like squirrels because they eat from bird feeders and scare away the birds; however, squirrels do a lot for their environment. Many an acorn or other seed stored and forgotten by a squirrel grows into a new tree, helping the forest continue to grow.

There is something so rascally and adorable about squirrels; maybe it's their great climbing ability, or the way they chase each other across lawns and up trees. Either way, squirrels are an animal that deserves a little attention.

What is a squirrel?

A squirrel is a member of the family Sciuridae. They are all rodents, like mice and capybaras, for example, but they are their own unique family. They include the squirrels you may see outside your window on a fall day, as well as chipmunks and flying squirrels.

A red squirrel sitting out in the snow.

But what defines a squirrel? For one example, most squirrels have big incisors (front teeth) that they use to crack open things like nuts. Then, there is a diastema (a space between the teeth) between the front and back teeth. The back teeth are designed to grind food.

Another thing they all have in common is being mammals; they have fur, many have climbing ability, and their babies are helpless. Their babies are hairless, blind, and with only gums, like human babies. They can't survive without their mothers.

Squirrels' fur is generally fairly silky, though some is less soft than others. They have long tails, and come in many different colors. Even if a squirrel is called red squirrel or a gray squirrel (which are two types of squirrels) they may be an entirely different color, such as black.

They have four or five toes on each foot, often including a thumb, though their thumb is not nearly as good as a human thumb. Tree squirrels also are some of the only animals to be able to climb down a tree face first; many animals can climb up a tree, such as cats, but it takes a certain sort of build to climb the way that tree squirrels do.

Squirrels have large eyes, and this gives them excellent vision; also, tree squirrels have tails that aid them in balancing, but they have been shown to be able to climb without them. Sometimes, predators will bite off their tails, and it doesn't seem to impede them, though their balance will never be quite the same.

They have varied diets. Squirrels can't digest cellulose, a major part of plants, so their diet usually depends more on things like nuts, seeds, and fungi. However, some sorts of squirrels will eat insects, and others have been known to eat meat (and things like eggs and baby animals) in desperation.

Spring is a very hard time for squirrels. Since they rely on mostly non-plants, there is not a lot available, and the nuts they've buried in the ground are often sprouting by then, making them useless as food for squirrels.

A young squirrel does not have a very good shot at making it past a year; the majority (most) of squirrels don't live past a year. Those that aren't killed by things like other animals, starvation, and cars live to about three to five years.

Squirrels reproduce about once or twice a year; females are left to take care of the babies on their own; after anywhere from six to ten weeks, the babies are weaned (made to be able to survive on normal food instead of their mother's milk) and they leave the nest. Squirrels are old enough to have their own babies at about a year old.

What kinds of squirrels are there?

There are many subfamilies of squirrels. They range from those from Asia (a couple of types with small variation) to the diversity of the tree squirrels and the terrestrial squirrels.

A marmot, which is a type of terrestrial squirrel.

There are also squirrels that are extinct today, from many thousands or even millions of years ago. Human beings had little, if anything, to do with these squirrels disappearing.

Interestingly, it seems like squirrels may have originated in North America, rather than in Africa. Because all the land was connected then, different types were able to spread to different continents; the only two continents that there aren't squirrels on are Australia and Antarctica.

Squirrels come in a number of subfamilies, as stated above. Some of the biggest groups are tree squirrels and terrestrial (ground) squirrels. These include marmots and chipmunks, for example, as well as red and gray squirrels that a lot of people see in places like Europe and

America. There are thirty-eight species of tree squirrels, but there are even more true flying squirrels: forty-five.

There's even one little subfamily that contains one type of squirrel: the neotropical pygmy squirrel, which is a very small type of squirrel. It's only about 10 centimeters in length, making it the smallest in the Americas.

Then there are the Oriental giant squirrels, which are the size of cats! They live in places like India and Southeast Asia, which includes places such as Cambodia and Thailand.

Where do squirrels live?

Squirrels live all over the world, from tropical rainforests to deserts, though they tend not to live in polar regions. There are squirrels that are very small, and then there are large ground squirrels that are much bigger.

An Eastern Flying Squirrel in a birdhouse.

In America, tree squirrels are most common, depending a lot on which part of America you're in; the same goes for Canada. Where there is a lot of flat land with no trees, that's where the terrestrial (or ground) squirrels live. This includes ground hogs, for example, who live in many areas in North America.

In Asia, there are many large squirrels and small squirrels; it's the biggest inhabited continent, so there's a lot of variety. Some live in forests, and some live in less forested areas.

There are even squirrels in Africa, where the smallest of squirrels lives, the African pygmy squirrel, which is around 7-10 centimeters.

The history of squirrels and humans

Squirrels have long been the food of humans. Not so much a popular food, such as beef or pork, but the desperate food of desperate humans. Squirrels were not the sort of food to serve to royalty or nobility in old times in Europe, for example. It's because, especially with European squirrels, there's not much meat on them to eat.

A squirrel eating from a bird feeder.

Nowadays, most people in first world countries (places like Germany, America, Canada, and the United Kingdom) don't eat squirrels. The main concern with squirrels of all kinds tends to be them intruding upon gardens and bird feeders.

In fact, it's sort of an obsession for some Americans. What squirrels see as an easy source of food, Americans see as a feeder to lure pretty birds into their yards. When the squirrel eats from it, it scares away the birds, and this makes Americans upset. Often, a lot of time is devoted to making the feeder so that only birds can feed from it.

Sometimes they have to put a large, plastic object shaped like a bowl above the feeder, so that the squirrels can't climb down whatever is holding the feeder up. Other times, they put tall, iron poles in the ground with hooks for feeders. Squirrels can't climb up these, since they don't have anything to grip.

Some people in other areas of America will hunt or trap squirrels. They have several reasons they might do this.

One thing that squirrels (particularly chipmunks and groundhogs) often do is eat the food in the garden. For example, a strawberry patch may be raided by chipmunks to the point that the person who planted them might not get any strawberries from their work.

Other reasons are the way that they may mess up the yard, such as in the case of the groundhog. A groundhog needs a place to live, and so they will dig or hide under the house or a shed in suburban areas.

So, often when someone catches something like a groundhog, they will release it in a park, far away from home.

It's recommended that, if you have a squirrel problem, to use a type of device that will emit a noise that bothers rodents; this will keep them at least out from under porches and sheds, and it's painless to the squirrels. It is never our right to be cruel.

What is a tree squirrel?

An easy definition is a squirrel who lives in trees, but it's a little more complex than that. Tree squirrels belong to the subfamily Sciurinae, as well as to the tribe Sciurini. They are in the same subfamily as true flying squirrels.

An eastern gray squirrel; this type of squirrel is native to America and Canada.

There are many different types of tree squirrels. Here are a few:

Eastern gray squirrel, also known simply as a gray squirrel. This is a common squirrel in America and Canada, to the Eastern side. It is one of the types that practices scatter hoarding, which means that it has many different spots where it stores its food. For instance, if it suddenly found a lot of food in one spot, it might bury as much as it could, and then move it to a safer location later.

Since so many squirrels die before one year of age, these caches, which include things like acorns, are often responsible for new trees.

Something that gray squirrels do is build nests in trees. These nests are made out of sticks and leaves, and they are called 'dreys.' Dreys are mostly used during cold weather, and gray squirrels may share them with other gray squirrels during this time. Dreys are also where they keep their babies.

Another type of tree squirrel is the red squirrel, also known as the Eurasian red squirrel. It lives in, as you might have guessed, Europe and Asia. It is not always red, especially not the further you get from Great Britain.

The red squirrel is generally a little smaller than the gray squirrel, who is has to compete with in Britain at least for resources. The gray squirrel was brought over, and has no natural predators, so it is a bit of a pest in places like England and Wales.

An interesting thing about the red squirrel is that males and females are the same size. There is very little difference between how males look and how females look.

Red squirrels are very good climbers; they can even climb house walls, and have been known to leap between trees. They also know how to swim. Like gray squirrels, they also make dreys.

The Mexican fox squirrel is another kind of tree squirrel. It lives in Mexico and also parts of the American state, Arizona. It sometimes lives in communal groups, and nests in dreys and hollow trees.

It's colored differently than, say, the gray or red squirrel, with a brown back, a yellowish to reddish tummy, and a dark tail.

Mexican fox squirrels are not really territorial, meaning that they don't defend the area they live in. They tend to react to a predator's presence by freezing and staying hidden among the underbrush and other plants. When they are a safe distance away, such as up in a tree, they may bark or throw things.

They don't hibernate during the winter, and they generally forage during the day and sleep during the night. When it comes to hiding food, they tend to bury it not in the dirt, but under the covering of things like dead leaves and such. However, they are less likely to do this than a gray squirrel, instead eating their food on the spot.

Not a lot is known about Mexican fox squirrels as compared to red and gray squirrels.

What is a true flying squirrel?

A true flying squirrel is a member of the Sciurinae subfamily, like the tree squirrels, but is a different tribe, called Pteromyini. The chief characteristic of true flying squirrels is the ability to glide through the air.

A baby flying squirrel.

A flying squirrel does not literally fly. Like a human on a hang glider, they don't use their own power to stay up in the air. Instead, they leap from high up and use their unique bodies to catch the air and glide.

One type of true flying squirrel is the red giant flying squirrel. This is an Asian species, stretching from Afghanistan all the way to Taiwan. It has been seen in places like Malaysia and Sri Lanka.

The red giant flying squirrel is a dark red color, except in places like around its eyes where it is black. It is very large, being almost a foot and a half long, which is around 420 millimeters.

It has the a thin piece of skin between each front leg and back leg, and this is what it uses to glide between trees. When it glides, it has been known to go up to 75 meters between leaping spot and landing spot.

The red giant flying squirrel lives on things like pine cones and other parts of conifer trees (which are a type of tree, including pines, that don't shed their leaves or needles in the fall). They also eat fruit and nuts, but only when these are in season.

It only has one or two babies at a time.

The Siberian flying squirrel is another type of true flying squirrel. It lives not just in Siberia, but also in places like Latvia, Estonia, and Finland. Its range stretches all the way to the Pacific coast.

The male Siberian flying squirrel tends to be just a little smaller than the female. They are both gray, and have very black eyes.

There is some concern in Europe that these squirrels may be endangered in their European habitat, especially since they are the only flying squirrels in Europe. However, they seem to be doing just fine in their mainly Russian habitat.

They are nocturnal, and feed on things such as cones, nuts, sprouts, and sometimes even eggs and baby birds. This is a sign the Siberian flying squirrel is omnivorous, or at least will eat almost anything to survive.

They do not hibernate during winter, and they have to avoid predators such as owls, cats, and martens.

Two types of flying squirrels, the only ones that live in North America, are the Northern and Southern flying squirrels, which are closely related to each other, though the Northern is larger.

Southern flying squirrels live from East Canada to the state of Florida in America. They have darker fur on top of their bodies, and a creamy color for the underside.

They eat mostly nuts and fruit, but like the Siberian flying squirrel, they have been known to eat eggs and baby birds. Other things they will eat include insects, mushrooms, and flowers.

A real threat to Southern flying squirrels are pet cats. Most cats will not hesitate to capture a flying squirrel, and many Southern flying squirrels die this way. Like most squirrel species, most don't make it past their first year.

The Northern flying squirrel is different in a number of ways. For one, where the Southern flying squirrel prefers deciduous (trees that lose their leaves) habitats, Northern ones prefer coniferous. Also, the Northern is nocturnal. Southern flying squirrels often live together in groups, Northern do not.

What is a terrestrial squirrel?

Terrestrial means ground, or earth, or belonging to the ground or earth. These types of squirrels live on and/or in the earth, rather than in trees. It covers a wide range of animals, but here are a few of the group in short.

A chipmunk, which is a type of terrestrial squirrel.

Most terrestrial squirrels belong to the subfamily Xerinae. A few of the squirrels in the family are in trees, but they aren't called terrestrial squirrels.

Chipmunks are one of the best known of this subfamily; all kinds of chipmunks, from the 23 North American kinds to the one Siberian chipmunk, have stripes running down their backs and cute black eyes.

They can climb trees, but in general, you are much more likely to see them on the ground, where they do most of their foraging. Like the tree squirrels and the flying squirrels, most of their diet is made up of nuts and other such things, and like their brothers and sisters, they will eat meat if they have to.

They also eat fungi, which helps to spread it throughout the forest or other area they live in.

Chipmunks make big burrows, with lots of little rooms. This is what makes them terrestrial squirrels, even though they can climb trees.

Unlike a lot of squirrel species, chipmunks tend to live to only three years at most, and many of them don't make it to that.

But in captivity, some chipmunks have lived to nine years, and they have been known to sleep a lot more than their wild brothers and sisters. It's guessed that this is because they realize there are no predators, and don't have to stay as alert.

A chipmunk will store all its food in its burrow, rather than scatter hoarding.

Marmots is a term that refers to ground hogs and other large squirrels that live on the ground. Marmots are creatures that tend to live in the mountains.

However, ground hogs are a kind of marmot that is often found in suburban areas, and they often annoy locals by eating garden produce and digging holes.

They dig burrows, and unlike most other squirrels, they tend to survive off of grasses and such. They also hibernate throughout the winter, sometimes in burrows dug into the dirt, and others in ones made of rock piles.

Like their cousin the prairie dog, they whistle to communicate, and are also fairly social, though not quite as much as the prairie dog.

What is an Oriental giant squirrel?

Oriental giant squirrels are squirrels the size of cats. They live in the South/Southeast Asia area, meaning areas like Thailand and Vietnam.

An Oriental giant squirrel.

One type of Oriental giant squirrel is the Indian giant squirrel, also known as the Malabar giant squirrel. It lives (you guessed it) in India. It can be reddish, creamy-colored, dark, or any combination of these colors or more. They always have a distinctive white spot between their ears.

It eats mainly fruit.

They can kind of look like monkeys, but these squirrels are definitely rodents.

The Indian giant squirrel is the opposite of the ground squirrel: it stays in the upper canopy of jungles or forests, and it rarely, if ever, touches the ground.

Scientists are not sure if there are many different subspecies of the Indian giant squirrel, but it comes in a lot of varieties. It is not endangered.

Conclusion

There are so many types of squirrels in the world, from the colorful to the plain, from the deepest parts of Africa to the farthest corners of Asia to farthest reaches of Canada. There are far more that aren't covered in this book.

Most squirrels are not endangered, and there is still so much we can learn about the jungle-dwelling squirrels. Maybe you'll be one of the ones who researches them; maybe you'll know someone who does.

If you've liked the squirrels in this book, you should go out and see if you can find some squirrels. In almost any forest, you're likely to spot at least one, if there's good weather.

Squirrels are here and here to stay; hopefully they won't mind sharing the world with us humans.

Author Bio

Rachel Smith is a young author who enjoys animals. Once, she had a rabbit who was very nervous, and chewed through her leash and tried to escape. She's also had several pet mice, who were the funniest little animals to watch. She lives in Ohio with her family and writes in her spare time.

Our books are available at
1. Amazon.com
2. Barnes and Noble
3. Itunes
4. Kobo
5. Smashwords
6. Google Play Books

Publisher

JD-Biz Corp

P O Box 374

Mendon, Utah 84325

http://www.jd-biz.com/

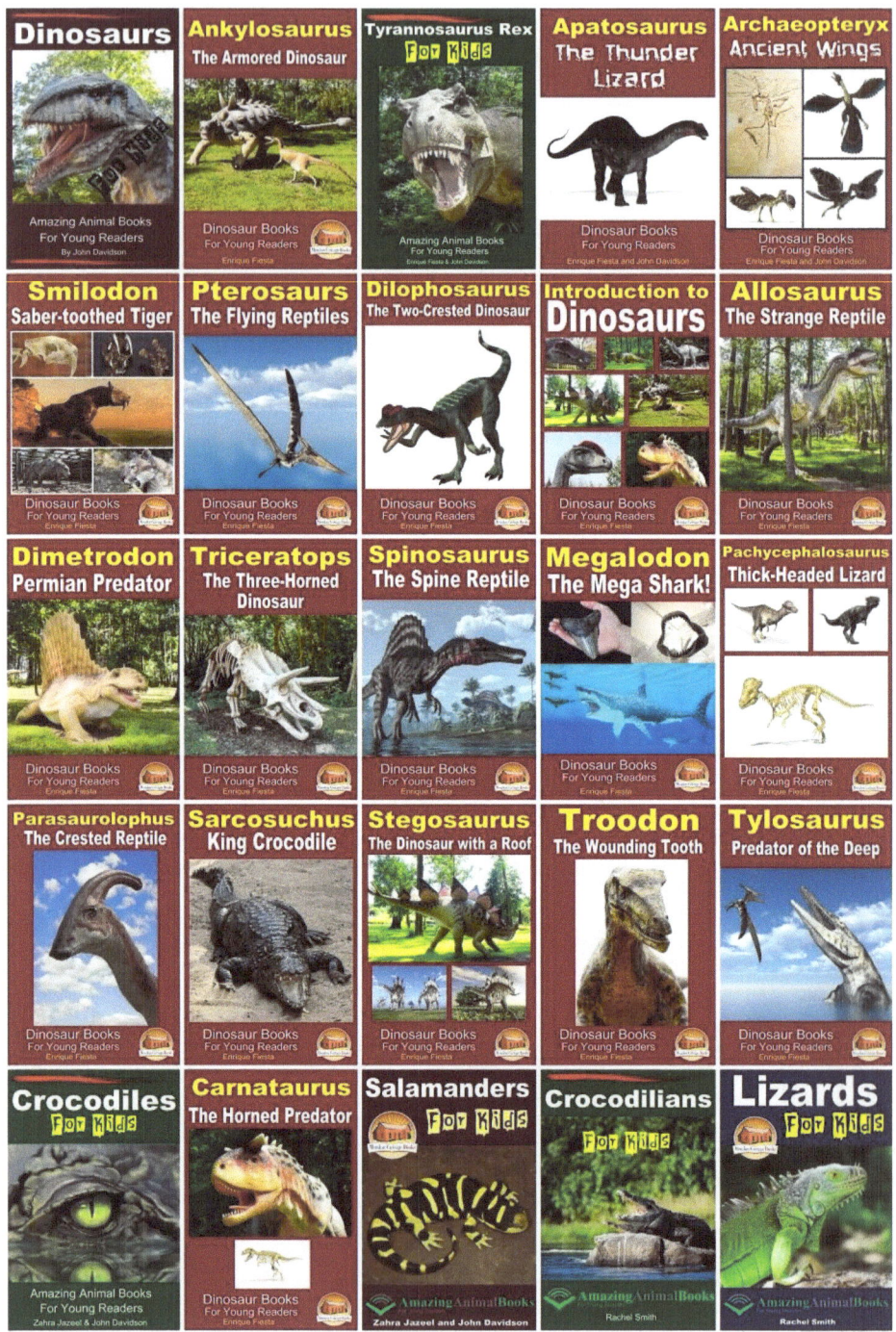